What others say a

Housecleaners' Program:

"I can't thank you enough for helping me get started. I almost didn't do it. Now I'm making four times the money I was making in fast food. The best part is that I'm the boss."

Sherry Netland
Phoenix, Arizona

"I never dreamed it would be so easy to start my own cleaning business. I just followed your program and in a few weeks had my first ten houses. I've met some really great people, and now I have two girls working for me. Thanks for everything."

Molly Irinage
Detroit, Michigan

"After my divorce I had to go back to work full-time for minimum wage. It's amazing how much my life has changed in such a short time since I got the program. I don't worry any more about where the money is going to come from to take care of my kids. If I can do it anyone can!"

Karen Yarnell
San Bernadino, California

"I recommend American Housecleaners' program to anyone who is trapped in a low paying job. I was surprised at first how many people are looking for someone to clean their houses. I just turned 19 years old and can't believe the money I'm making for something I have always done for free. This program is everything you said it was!"

Becky Castalana
Columbus, Ohio

"I have to admit I was a little skeptical about your program at first, but after I tried some of the techniques to find clients my confidence increased. Thanks to you I have more work than I know what to do with. My clients really depend on me and the money is great."

Michelle Grattam
Houston, Texas

American Housecleaners' Guide™ to Starting Your Own Housecleaning Business

Second Edition

Rae Ann Luethy

McGraw-Hill, Inc.
College Custom Series

New York St. Louis San Francisco Auckland Bogotá Caracas Lisbon London Madrid Mexico Milan Montreal New Delhi Paris San Juan Singapore Sydney Tokyo Toronto

American Housecleaners' Guide™ to Starting Your Own Housecleaning Business

2 3 4 5 6 7 8 9 0 BKM BKM 9 0 9 8 7 6 5

ISBN 0-07-049387-1

Editor: Julie Kehrwald
Printer/Binder: Bookmart Press

Contents

Introduction

I feel as though I'm sitting on a gold mine. I know a way that anybody, regardless of background, experience or resources, can make excellent money while doing a job that is easy, fun, satisfying, and that has many side benefits. The secret is to start your own housecleaning business, and I know that anybody can do it, because I did it myself.

Some years ago I was an inexperienced 18-year-old without any special training or financing. In fact, it was all I could do to scrape up enough cash to buy a pizza! But I had a desire to be independent and make good money. I got the idea of starting my own housecleaning business.

With the rashness of youth, I put an ad in the paper, and got over 75 calls from it! Before I knew it I had a full schedule and the money was rolling in. Not only that, but before long I realized how easy the job was. Sure, the first time you clean a house it takes a little longer. But once you've cleaned a house really well a few times, and you're doing that house on a regular basis, you only need to do surface cleaning. You hardly even get messed up. It came to a point where I could clean a house in the morning and then go meet a friend for lunch, and no one would guess I'd been working at all. From the way I was dressed, I could have been out playing tennis.

The other amazing thing I discovered was that cleaning houses could actually be a glamorous profession. You get to meet interesting and wealthy people. For years I cleaned houses in Southern California where my clientele included Hollywood actors and other celebrities. I often had opportunities to help out at exciting dinner parties and house-sit in luxurious summer homes. Wealthy customers frequently gave me gifts of china and furniture as they bought new things for themselves. I was running around with a whole new circle of friends and experiencing a completely different lifestyle, just because one day I got tired of working in a dead-end job at minimum wage and decided to take my future into my own hands.

Now, I have to admit that at the beginning I did make some mistakes. The first time I cleaned a house it took me eight hours when it should only have taken me two. But I have learned so much since then, that I feel compelled to write this. You won't have to make the same mistakes I did or go through the whole learning process because in the pages of this guide I have written down everything you need to know to be an instant success. I will teach you how to find clients, how to determine how much to charge for your work and how to clean a house the easy way.

It's my nature to always try to do things the fastest, most efficient way. Over the years I have developed a system of cleaning that works in any size or type of home. This method is described in detail here. If you master this cleaning system, and anybody can, you'll find that cleaning a house is a pleasant, easy and quick process. You'll be amazed and delighted with the results - and you'll be delighted with the money you'll be making as well.

I'm very excited about this guide and I know you will be too. It can open the door to a whole new career for you. I know that with the step-by-step instructions and special hints you'll find in this book, along with your own enthusiasm and willingness to try something new, you'll "clean-up" in this business. In fact, you can't miss!

Rae Ann Luethy

CHAPTER ONE

The Business of Housecleaning

WHY should you be interested in starting your own business as a housecleaner? Well, how would you feel about a job that offered you the following?:

Excellent Pay
Flexible Hours
Immediate Cash
Easy, Pleasant Work
Opportunity To Meet Interesting People
No Special Training Or Experience Required
No Start-up Expenses

It sounds ideal doesn't it? Every one of the above-mentioned benefits applies. Now you know why you should start your own housecleaning business.

As a professional housecleaner you can make \$35-\$50 every time you clean a house (or more depending on the size of the house). Since you can use the cleaning system described in this book to clean a house in 2 to 3 hours, you'll be making up to \$25 an hour.

Since you're the boss, you can arrange your schedule the way you like it. Work mornings only if you like. Work every day or every other day. Need a lot of money quickly? Take on some extra work for a few weeks or months. Plan everything to suit yourself.

You'll get paid every day for the work you've done that day. The cash or check will be in your hands to spend immediately, as you like.

The work is easy. Keeping a house clean is a snap after you've done the basic deep cleaning once or twice. Your regular houses will require surface cleaning only, with no hard scrubbing called for. It's healthy to be active and move around, and soon you'll look on cleaning a house as light exercise. If you start taking on jobs in wealthy neighborhoods you'll find yourself meeting all sorts of interesting people, and there will be many benefits from that. First, other opportunities for special jobs may present themselves. You might be asked to help out at elegant dinner parties. Sometimes a client may need someone to house-sit for awhile and you could find yourself living rent-free in a charming summer house in the mountains or on the beach. Wealthy people often buy new things and are generous in giving away what they don't need anymore. Clothes, furniture, dishes. I personally have received a wide variety of gifts that I still treasure.

Best of all, anybody can start a housecleaning business. Male or female, any age or background anyone can do it. You don't have to go to school or get any special training. You don't even have to have any money to get started. The most you might need is a few dollars to put a small classified ad in the paper. The client will furnish all your cleaning supplies so you don't even have to be concerned about that. Just invest a little time to study this program, and you'll know everything you need to know to become a professional in no time at all.

BUT, IS THERE A MARKET FOR HOUSECLEANERS?

Now, more than ever, people need help caring for their homes. Think of all the two-career families there are. People are exhausted after a tension-filled day at the office. The last thing they want to have to do is vacuum or clean the bathroom. And yet everyone likes to come home to a clean house that is a comfortable and relaxed retreat from the world outside. And what about the single parent, maybe recently divorced? This may be a perfect opportunity for offering your cleaning services.

If you have any doubt about how many people are looking for reliable help, just put an ad in the paper. You'll be amazed at how many responses you'll get. The question won't be "Will I be able to find work?" The question will be, "How much time am I willing to give to my new career?"

HOW MUCH MONEY CAN I MAKE?

The amount of money you can make depends entirely on how much time you're willing or able to devote to your business. If you just want to earn a little extra spending money, work a couple of mornings a week. If you want a real career, work full time. You'll be making a minimum of $35 to $50 for every house you clean. Once you've mastered the cleaning techniques described here you'll be able to do a house easily in 2 to 3 hours. At two houses a day, five days a week, you'll be making $450 every week, $1800 every month, close to $22,000 every year - and that's without any training or outlay of money on your part. And you're only working 4 to 6 hours each day. Imagine what you could do with an employee or two.

If you schedule houses located close together on the same day, and if you are really ambitious, you can earn even more. If you had 3 houses located in the same neighborhood, you could make $120 or more in one day, working 6 to 8 hours. Where else could you make money like that? And remember, since you're the boss, you can expand or cut back at any time you want.

LICENSING

Licensing your housecleaning business is a good idea. In fact, by doing so you will establish immediate credibility and can include the fact that you are licensed in your advertising. Contact your town clerk or city hall to register the name and existence of your housecleaning business. The fee for licensing will usually vary between $10 and $75 annually.

BONDING AND INSURANCE

Most homeowners carry their own insurance that will cover you while cleaning their home, however, being bonded further protects you and can only add to your credibility. Being bonded is relatively inexpensive. You can purchase a $5,000 bond for $100. Check with your local insurance agent to help determine your needs.

TAKE THE FIRST STEP

You've now been given information that should convince you that starting your own housecleaning business is something you would enjoy and that would be very easy for you to do.

The rest of this guide will give you step-by-step instructions for every phase of the business. Reading and studying this material will be the first step to a whole new occupation for you that will be both lucrative and personally satisfying. Follow the path outlined here, and it will take you as far as you want to go.

CHAPTER TWO

Your First Lesson: How to Act Like a Professional

CLEANING houses is easy. But there's a little more to being a success as a housecleaner than just knowing how to clean a house. As your first lesson in being a professional housecleaner, let's look at what you have to know to maintain a professional manner. There are two reasons why you need to learn this. First, you have to present yourself in such a way that the client feels confident that you are willing, and able, to do the job to her satisfaction. You have to be the kind of person people feel comfortable allowing into their homes, usually while they are not there to watch you. The way you present yourself will be an important factor in getting, and keeping your clients. Second, you want to learn certain points about being a professional so that you always stay in control of the situation. You don't want to be manipulated into doing more than you're getting paid for. Sometimes you have to be able to draw the line, and therefore the relationship you develop with your client is very important. So before we go into the how-to's of starting and running your housecleaning business, let's look at some of these more personal matters first.

MAINTAINING A PROFESSIONAL APPEARANCE

When you go to clean a house you have to look like you're serious about your job. You are not there to impress the client with your wardrobe or skill as a make-up artist. I remember one time when I was first starting out, I went to meet a client who told me she had just interviewed a young woman who had beautifully manicured, long fingernails. She told me that she laughed to herself when she saw this would-be housecleaner because she wondered if she'd be more concerned with getting the shower clean or chipping her nail polish. Because I looked more willing to do a good job she gave me a chance and hired me. Little details, like how your fingernails look, can turn out to be very important.

My advice is to wear clean, comfortable clothes that are easy to work in. I personally prefer sweats and a t-shirt because they don't bind at all. Avoid anything low-cut or showy, and don't wear anything that you'll be afraid to get cleaning solution on. Come dressed so you can work without any concern for what you're wearing. This means you should forget the fancy hairdos and manicured nails. Save them for your evenings out and leisure time.

There's also a little psychology to keep in mind here. You don't want the lady of the house to feel threatened by your glamorous appearance. Let her be the queen in her own castle. Also, I suggest if the husband is home, you say a friendly, business-like hello, and then ignore him. Women can be very jealous, and depending on what the situation is between the husband and wife, it may not take much provocation for you to be seen as a danger. By the same token, if you are a man going into the cleaning business, be careful that you don't make a female client feel uncomfortable by being flirtatious. Just be casual, friendly and business-like. It will avoid difficulties later on.

MAINTAINING A PROFESSIONAL RELATIONSHIP WITH YOUR CLIENT

Sometimes there's a tendency to get overly familiar with people, but try to avoid getting too friendly with your clients. This doesn't mean you aren't pleasant and accommodating. But it does mean you don't want to start sharing personal secrets, gossiping about other people or doing personal favors. People don't like to pay their friends, or take money from them. If you start getting too close to your clients they may start expecting special jobs without paying for them. And you may hesitate to ask to get paid what you deserve.

Also remember that friendships sometimes fade. If that happens you and your client won't feel comfortable with each other anymore and you could easily lose the house. What's worse, your ex-client, ex-friend could reveal things about you to your other clients, or be afraid that you could reveal things about her. Wouldn't it be better to avoid these potential problems altogether? Keep your personal life separate from your business life, and both will be happier.

SUMMARY

Here are the two main points you should remember about acting like a professional housecleaner:

1. Maintain a professional appearance. Dress like someone who is serious about cleaning houses.

2. Maintain a professional relationship with your client. Be friendly and pleasant, but don't develop too personal a relationship.

Remember these rules and all your interactions with your clients will be easy.

CHAPTER THREE

Finding that House: The Art of Advertising

BECOMING a professional housecleaner is very easy. It only takes one thing. Finding a house that someone will pay you to clean! To find that house you have to let people know you're looking for it. Welcome to the world of advertising.

You don't need a lot of money to advertise. A little imagination and enthusiasm go a long way, and there are many things you can do that cost little or nothing. Newspaper ads, calling on the telephone and going door-to-door are all good methods that can help you find a house to clean fast. Your situation and personality will determine which way is the best for you.

Let's look at several methods you can use that will help you find that house!

NEWSPAPER ADS

An ad in the local newspaper is one of the quickest and best ways to find a house to clean. This method will work for you if you have a little extra money, maybe $15 to $25, to pay for the ad. You will also need reliable transportation. After all, you could get calls from anywhere in the distribution area of the paper, and you want to be sure you can reach your house once you've found it.

One advantage of a newspaper ad is that you can reach a large number of people in a widespread area with little effort. Your ad does all the work. Also, you can be certain that the people who respond to your ad are definitely looking for a professional housecleaner and will be willing to pay for the service.

Your ad will cost you money, so you want to make sure you get the most out of it. Check to see which newspapers are distributed in your target area. There might be a large daily paper, a smaller local weekly, and a "shopper" which only publishes ads. Pick the one you think is most likely to be read by your potential customers. Call the advertising departments of these papers to find out what the rates are for a "classified ad". (Some papers have all the information and an application printed in the section where they run the ads.) To make sure that you get results from your ad, plan to run it for at least one week, and maybe even for two. Ask the clerk in the advertising department if there is a special rate for running the ad longer. You will probably be charged by the word or line for your classified ad, so look at your budget to determine how big an ad you can buy.

Now that you've selected a newspaper and determined the size of your ad, you're ready to write it. You want something short and to the point that will attract attention and leave the impression that you are someone worth calling. Look at other ads in the paper and see what catches your eye. If you've noticed the same ad being run over a long period of time, chances are that it has worked well for the advertiser. Make sure your ad has all the vital facts (like your phone number), and put in some words that will inspire confidence, like "reliable", "dependable", "reasonable".

Your ad could read:

"Housecleaning. Honest. Reliable. Reasonable Free Estimates. Call 555-0000."

Or,

"Housecleaning you can thoroughly depend on. 555-0000."

Expressions like "sparkling clean, experienced" and "professional" add to the power of your ad.

You will be putting a phone number in your ad so people can reach you, so try to be available to answer the phone when they call. It would be best if you could answer the phone yourself. If you (or someone you trust) cannot be at the phone all the time, an answering machine or a voicemail system might be the solution. Make whatever arrangements are necessary, because when someone responds to your ad, you want her to know you're glad she called. (By the way, in most cases your client will be a woman, so throughout this guide I'll refer to "her" in order to simplify things. Of course, everything will apply to male clients as well.)

THE TELEPHONE / REVERSE DIRECTORY

Another way to let people know that you're available to clean houses is to call them on the telephone. This method is virtually free, and gives you more control over the type of people you will be reaching than a newspaper ad does. You can use a regular telephone book to find people to call, but a reverse directory is better. A reverse directory lists people according to the street they live on (rather than by name), so you can pinpoint exactly the area in which you want to find your house. This is very helpful if you have a problem with transportation because you can make sure you only call people who are within walking distance of where you live. You can find a reverse directory in most libraries. You won't be able to check it out, but you can make copies.

The best thing to do when using a reverse directory is to find a nice area near your house, neighborhoods that you think hire housecleaners. Drive around and write down all the street names in that area. Then go to the library and ask to look at their reverse directory. Find the streets that you wrote down and make copies of them. This way you will know the area already and once you get one house in that area it will be easier for you to get other ones. You will be able to say "I clean Mrs. Jones' house down the street." I prefer the reverse directory method because it allows you to get homes in the area of your choice and doesn't cost any money.

Some people are a little hesitant about calling strangers on the phone, but really it's not that hard to do. Once you've made the first few calls it will get easier and easier, and you might even find that you enjoy it. Keep in mind that there are people out there who really would like a housecleaner. This is a fast-paced world and people with hectic schedules will welcome the idea that someone could help them with the burden of maintaining their homes. Everyone likes to come home to a clean house. So keep a positive attitude.

It's also important to prepare yourself ahead of time. Give some thought to what you will say. Try your pitch out on a friend if possible.

While you're calling have some index cards handy so you can take notes.

Okay. You've got your cards and pen, and you know what you want to say. You've picked the area in the reverse directory you want to cover, or you've decided just to start with the A's in the regular telephone book. You're ready to go, so just start dialing.

When the phone rings and someone answers, you should try to sound friendly and businesslike. Start with something like this: "Hello, (Mr. or Mrs. ________) my name is Mary Johnson. I do housecleaning in the area and wanted to know if I could stop by and give you a free estimate." You will most likely end up dealing with the woman of the house, but at this point ask your question to whoever answers the phone. Of course, if a very young child answers ask to speak to their mother or father. It's funny, but teenagers always seem to think their mothers will be interested in hiring a housecleaner, even if she turns out not to be interested at all. Maybe they are the ones who would like a little help with their chores, but nevertheless, it's usually the mother who will hire you.

Now is the time to start taking notes. It is very important that you be organized because you are now developing your list of customer leads that will be extremely valuable to you later on. If you don't write things down immediately you may not remember them later.

First, keep track of the section in the telephone book or reverse directory you've covered so you don't keep calling the same people. If you find some people who are definitely not interested, you should put a line by their names in your book.

Start a separate index card on anyone who is interested in your service. Even if they don't want someone right now they might say something like: "I've been thinking of hiring someone but not for a few months." This is someone you definitely want to call back. Write down on your index card the person's name, address, telephone number, the date you called her, and the date when you are supposed to call her again.

Even if the person you call says, "No, I'm not interested," this does not have to be the end of the conversation. After you've become more comfortable working on the phone you might get brave and ask, "Do you do the cleaning yourself?" If she says that she has a housecleaner who comes in, you will want to make a note of this. Here is a person who does use the services of someone like yourself and is therefore a potential customer. You could call her back at a later time to see if she's still happy with her cleaner, or if she might be interested in hiring someone else. The good notes you've taken now will pay off tremendously in the future. You will have a record of good future prospects that can save you a lot in advertising fees.

Remember while you're calling that many people have had bad experiences with housecleaners in the past. You want to sound like someone who can be trusted to be businesslike, honest and pleasant. If you are calling from the reverse directory to a house in your neighborhood it might help to let the person know that you live nearby. If someone is looking for a housecleaner, and you sound like the kind of person she would feel confident to have come into her home, you will most likely be able to arrange an interview, and get the job.

Your ultimate goal in making phone calls is to arrange a time when you can visit the house to give an estimate. At that time, or maybe even while you're still on the phone, you will probably be asked what you charge, what your service includes and other more specific questions. We'll go into this in detail in the next chapter, "Turning a Potential Customer into Your Client."

GOING DOOR-TO-DOOR

If you like to get out in the open air and meet people face-to-face, then going door-to-door may be the best way to find your house. This can take more time than the other methods, but it costs you nothing and you can choose the exact location in which you want to work.

Like phone calling, going door-to-door can be difficult at the beginning. But once you've called on a few houses it gets easier. Just keep your goal in mind and remember how little it is costing you.

Actually, going door-to-door can have big advantages as far as getting hired. It is much more personal than any of the other methods. People can judge you by your friendly, neat appearance, and if they are interested you can look through the house right then and there.

Plan to go door-to-door in a neighborhood where the residents seem likely to employ housecleaners. You want to select an area that has nicer homes, but you should consider the size of the houses too. An exclusive area may have very large houses that would require too much work for the money. It might be best to stay with an average-sized house in a nice neighborhood.

When going door-to-door you will need to be able to take good notes, just as you did with phone calling. This will be the key to continuing to get new jobs. Bring a notebook and a pen or pencil so you can write down the name and address of anyone who shows an interest in your service. Get the phone number too, if possible. You should also be prepared to give your potential customer a business card with your name and phone number. But you don't need to invest in professional business cards. You can just take a sheet of paper and write your name and number on it about 10 times, spaced evenly. Then go to a printing shop or business service and have some sheets photocopied. Cut the sheets up into nice little "cards," and you're ready to go.

The first thing to do is to walk up to the door and ring the bell or knock. Don't be overly aggressive, but don't be too timid either. You want to be friendly and businesslike.

When someone answers the door you can say something like,

> *"Hello, my name is Mary. I do housecleaning in this area and I was wondering if you'd be interested in a free estimate."*

If she says she is interested you can go on to the next step. But even if she says she is not interested you can still pursue things a little further. Ask her if she does her own cleaning or if she uses a housecleaning service. If she says she does her own cleaning, give her one of your "cards" and say,

> *"Here is my phone number. If you find you need some help during the holidays, or if an emergency comes up, feel free to call me."*

If she says, "I already have a housecleaning service," tell her,

> *"Here is my phone number. If your housecleaner gets sick or moves and you need someone at the last minute, please feel free to call me."*

Be glad if someone says she has a housecleaner. She is your potential customer. And if she loses her housecleaner she won't need to look in the newspaper for a new one if she has already met you!

It is very important that you keep good notes on the houses you visit. When you get back home transfer your notes onto separate index cards.

Write down the name, address and phone number of everyone who was interested, and put down a date when you should call again. Timing is very important. If you call exactly when someone is looking for a housecleaner, you will get the job.

FLYERS

Another technique you can combine with the door-to-door method is to use flyers.

Make up a flyer similar to the newspaper ad we discussed earlier. Type it up or print neatly, and have it photocopied or quick-printed onto brightly-colored paper.

Now when you go door-to-door, if no one is home you can leave a flyer with your message in the door. You can also post flyers on the public bulletin boards that you find in grocery stores or laundromats, choosing places often visited by the residents in your target area. Take a couple of hours and get your flyers out there.

Flyers take a small outlay of money, but they enable you to cover an area thoroughly. Just make sure they don't end up blowing into the street. Don't put flyers into Mail Boxes, as this is illegal, and check to see if there are any local rules about flyers that you need to follow.

WORD OF MOUTH

You'd be amazed at how quickly word spreads. Word of mouth can work wonders for you if you just start the ball rolling. The more people who know you are looking for houses to clean, the more likely that someone will mention that fact to someone else. So don't be afraid to tell everyone you know, including your clients, that you're looking for more houses to clean.

People are sometimes hesitant to hire strangers. They are always more comfortable hiring someone who is known by someone they know. Present yourself as a decent, pleasant and hardworking individual that others would be happy to recommend. Always ask for referrals. You'll soon have more houses than you know what to do with.

CONCLUSION

Of all the methods we've discussed for finding a house, advertising in the paper brings the quickest results. So, if you have a little money to place an ad, by all means do so. The next best method is to use the reverse directory to call potential clients in a specified area. Door knocking works well if you have some extra time or would like to get another house near one that you already enjoy cleaning. Word of mouth works for you all the time.

Remember, the most important things for you to do to find a house to clean is to let people know that you're available. There are several time-proven methods you can use that will cost you little or nothing. Starting can sometimes be the hardest part, but others have gotten over that first barrier and have developed successful, rewarding careers. You can too!

SUMMARY

Easy Ways to Find a House to Clean

1. Design and place an ad in the newspaper.
   a. Keep the ad short and to the point.
   b. Be available to answer calls from those who respond to your ad, or make other arrangments such as an answering machine or voice mail.

2. Call on the telephone / reverse directory.
   a. Find names in your local telephone book,or better yet use a reverse directory.
   b. Be organized and take notes.

3. Go door-to-door.
   a. Present a neat and pleasant appearance.
   b. Be organized.

4. Flyers.
   a. Works well with door-to-door technique.
   b. Post on public bulletin boards.

5. Word of mouth
   a. Your good reputation works for you.
   b. Ask for referrals.

CHAPTER FOUR

Turning a Potential Customer Into Your Client

NOW that you've let people know you're available to clean houses, they are going to start asking you questions. The way you respond to those questions is very important. You want to show them that you're confident, friendly, knowledgeable and trustworthy.

What kinds of questions will you get? The same kind you would ask. Do you work alone? What do you charge? Do you bring your own cleaning supplies? How old are you? How long have you been cleaning? Do you have any references? What does your cleaning include? You'll be able to answer these questions easily if you've prepared yourself ahead of time and know what you want to say.

You will also need to ask the customer some questions. After all, you can't give a reasonable estimate if you don't know how big the customer's house is.

Whether you're responding to a phone call or talking to a person you've met going door-to-door, the conversation will probably go pretty much the same. As an example, let's say you've put an ad in the paper. Mrs. A has seen the ad and wants to find out more about you, so she calls you.

(Phone rings. You answer.)

You: Hello.

Mrs. A: Hi. I'm calling about your housecleaning ad in the newspaper. Are you the one that does the cleaning?

You: Yes, I am.

Mrs. A: Well, could you please tell me what you charge?

You: Yes, most of my homes range from $35 to $50, depending on what you want done. If you can tell me the floor plan of your house, I can give you a general idea. Then if you're interested we can make an appointment so I can look at your house and tell you exactly what it would cost.

Mrs. A: I have four bedrooms and two and a half baths, a small kitchen and a family room.

You: How many bare floors do you have that would have to be mopped?

Mrs. A: I have a kitchen floor and a small entry way.

You: Is it a one or two-story house?

Mrs. A: Two story.

(This would probably be a $35 to $50 job. You don't want to say a figure that is too high, or she won't invite you over for the complete estimate. But if you say a figure that is too low, she won't want to pay the higher amount you quote her after actually seeing the house. Stay somewhere in the middle.)

You: That sounds like it might be a $40 job, give or take $5.

Mrs. A: Can you tell me what exactly your cleaning includes?

(After you've studied the chapter on "How To Clean A House Like A Professional" you'll be able to answer this question with ease. You'll probably say something like the following.)

You: I clean the bathrooms thoroughly, dust, do the glasswork, clean the kitchen including wiping down the countertops and cleaning and shining the outside of all the appliances. Then I vacuum or sweep the bare floors and clean them the way you normally would. Finally I vacuum all the carpets. This is the basic service. If you want anything else done we can discuss it when I come to your house to give an estimate.

Mrs. A: Do you bring your own cleaning supplies?

You: No. I like to use the brand each of my clients prefers. I will work with you and use the products you like.

(By this time Mrs. A is convinced that you know what you're talking about. Now you can move on to the next stage.)

You: Why don't we set up a time when I can meet you and give you a more complete estimate? When would it be convenient for you?

Mrs. A: I'll be home all afternoon. Can you come by today around 3:00?

You: I'd be happy to. Give me your address, and directions to your house, and I'll see you then.

Now wasn't that easy? When you know your cleaning method and have an idea of what to charge, you can feel confident talking to anyone. No one will be able to intimidate you. It is your cleaning business and you are the expert. But you should also remember that you want this woman to invite you into her house, so be friendly and cooperative too.

During your conversation with Mrs. A you should be preparing an index card on her (or adding to the one you started earlier). This card is very important to you. It lets you keep track of all your clients and potential clients. You will take the card with you on your first visit to the client's house and will use it to note down all the special things you have to remember about her. You might even want to have two cards on each client so you can keep one on file all the time, and carry one with you to the house. Be sure to write down on the card the directions to your client's house and the date and time of your appointment. Your card should have all these facts.

Name:
Telephone:
Address:
Directions to house:
Date and time of estimate:
Amount of estimate:
Special instructions:

Your customer may ask to see some references. Tell her, "I will be happy to give you references at the time I estimate your house." Be prepared to give her the names of some people who can vouch for your character and work. You should ask your references ahead of time if you can use their names.

Try to set up your appointment to give an estimate as soon as possible. You may not be the only person Mrs. A is calling. She may be a little nervous about interviewing people and will want to get it over with quickly. If you are the most willing and businesslike person she talks to, you will be the one to get the job. Be courteous and professional, and you will have no problem turning a potential customer into your client.

SUMMARY

How to Turn a Potential Customer Into Your Client

1. Appear confident, friendly, knowledgeable and trustworthy.
2. Offer a rough estimate that is neither too high nor too low.
3. Know your cleaning method.
4. Be prepared to give references.
5. Set up an appointment as soon as possible to meet the client and give a complete estimate.

CHAPTER FIVE

How to Clean a House Like a Professional

WHEN we finished Chapter 4 we were just getting ready to go over to Mrs. A's house to give her a complete estimate. But let's not rush over too soon. Before you can accurately estimate how much time and effort will be required to clean her house, you will need to know exactly what the cleaning process involves. When you go to speak to Mrs. A you want to know very clearly what needs to be done so that (l) you will make a good impression on her, and (2) you will not over or underestimate the job. If you quote her too high a price Mrs. A may decide to hire someone else. If you quote her too low a price you will be the one who will continue to get paid less than you deserve every time you go out to her house, which does not make for a cheery worker. Let's avoid these problems by learning right now how to clean a house. Then when we go over to meet Mrs. A we will be confident, knowledgeable and enthusiastic.

THE SYSTEM

People are often amazed at how quickly I can clean their homes. I can be in and out of a house in record time, and everything is immaculate, shined to a high finish, and nothing is overlooked. What is my secret?

The secret to cleaning a house like a professional is organization. Years of experience have enabled me to develop a "system" of cleaning that can be adapted to any house. This system permits the most efficient use of time and energy, with no back-tracking, fumbling for supplies or wasting time deciding what to do next.

In order to make good money as a housecleaner you have to learn to use your time to full advantage. This does not mean that you have to work fast. It means that you have to learn to work efficiently. An efficient worker moving at a nice, steady pace will accomplish much more in a limited amount of time than someone who tears around a house without any plan at all. "Slow and steady wins the race" is a good rule to follow in housecleaning, just as it is in most other areas of life.

A major time-waster we want to avoid is stopping to think. What should I do next? Did I remember to do that? Would it be better to do this or that first? All this can be eliminated when you approach a house with my system. This system can be adapted to any size house, and once you have learned how to use it you will approach any cleaning job with confidence. When you first start working in a new house it may take one or two times to get the system running perfectly. One thing you have to do, for example, is learn the best places to plug in the vacuum. Once you've adapted the system to a particular house, however, do not deviate from your plan, and you will always clean it in the most efficient way.

Here are the two major rules of the system that you should always follow:

1. *Always work from the top down.*
2. *Always do like jobs at the same time.*

Always Work From The Top Down.

It is very tiring and frustrating to have to clean the same spot over and over. But this is exactly what people have to do when they move dirt back onto a place they've just cleaned. As a simple example, if you dust the furniture after you've swept the floor, you will be dropping new dirt on top of your clean floor, and now you have to start all over. Always working from the top down eliminates this problem.

Always Do Like Jobs At The Same Time.

You always work more smoothly when you don't break your rhythm. However, most people make the mistake of cleaning a whole room at once, regardless of the smaller jobs this involves. If you dust the living room, and then stop to vacuum it, you're breaking your flow. Then you have to move everything to the next room and return to the first task. You will work more quickly and do a better job if you do all your dusting at one time. The vacuuming will come later. If you've been cleaning the other way all your life this may seem a little strange at first, but I know that this system works, and you can prove it for yourself.

As we go on to study the system in detail you will see how these rules are applied over and over. Master these rules, and you will be able to cut any job down to size.

Let's now go on to study the basic steps to always follow when cleaning a house with my system.

THE CLEANING PROCESS

You are now ready to begin cleaning. To start off collect all the supplies you will be using throughout the house. I have found it very handy to carry these supplies in a bucket which can then be used to rinse the showers and tubs. You will also need to have a trash bag with you that is big enough to hold all the trash you collect as you empty the baskets from room to room.

Here is our ground plan for attacking the house. We are going to start with the bathrooms and work our way toward the kitchen, saving all the floors for last.

These are the steps, in order, that we will follow:

1. *Clean all the bathrooms (except for the floors).*
2. *Dust.*
3. *Do the glasswork.*
4. *Clean the kitchen (except for the floor).*
5. *Do all the bare floors.*
6. *Vacuum the carpets.*

Keep this procedure in mind as we look at specific instructions for each job.

BATHROOMS

Always start a house by cleaning the bathrooms. This will be the case whether it is a one or two-story house. In a two story house, begin in the upstairs bathrooms.

The first thing you should do when you enter the bathroom is open the windows and turn on the lights. Good ventilation is essential when using chemicals of any kind, and, of course, you need to see what you're doing.

Now, put your bowl cleaner into the toilet bowl and leave it. The longer the solution sits in the bowl the easier it will be to clean later.

In order to clean thoroughly and quickly, all your surfaces should be clear of objects. Start in the shower area, removing all soaps, razors, shampoo bottles, etc. Set everything on the floor, far enough away from you so you won't be stepping over them repeatedly. Place the soap and other wet items on a paper towel so you won't stain the floor. Go on to remove all articles from the sink area, again placing them on the floor where they won't be in the way. Try to keep them in the same order in which you found them so they won't be rearranged when you put them back. Remove items from the top of the toilet bowl tank in the same way.

Now that all the surfaces are clear you can begin cleaning without any interference. Start by filling the sink with your chosen disinfectant cleaner, diluting it to the proper strength. Move first to the shower area and clean the inside from top to bottom. Do the shower doors, door runners and chrome.

Tip: Door runners can be cleaned easily if you use an old toothbrush and a rag.

Go on to clean the outside of the tub or shower, including any chrome. Once you've thoroughly wiped the entire area with your solution and everything is clean, you are ready to rinse. Thorough rinsing is as important as the cleaning itself. To rinse, turn on the shower head or faucet. Removable shower heads are great for rinsing, if you are lucky enough to have one at your disposal. If not, your bucket can be a big help too. Guide all the rinse water into the drain. Keep running your hand over the surfaces to check for grit and leftover residue as you rinse.

Now that the shower is clean, the next step is to clean the toilet. Again, clean it from top to bottom. Start from the top of the tank and work downward along the sides. Clean both sides of the seat and the outside of the bowl. Knobs and hinges, which can be easily overlooked, often gather dirt and residue. To do a professional job you want to make sure all this unsightly dirt is completely removed. A toothbrush is a very effective cleaning aid here. Use it well and the bowl will look like new.

Clean the inside of the toilet bowl last. If at all possible, avoid using a brush made of wire, because a worn wire brush can permanently scratch the inside of the bowl. I don't normally like to make suggestions to the customer about what supplies to provide, but in this case, if a wire brush was all that was available, I would suggest to the customer that she buy something else.

Now that you have finished the bowl, it is time to move on to the countertops. Clean them thoroughly with the cleaning solution that is still sitting in the sink, making sure you wipe the edges of the counter top. When you are satisfied that all is clean, rinse the area. Now you can empty the sink and clean it. Abrasives are usually safe for most sinks, but use them with caution on countertops as they can take off the finish when used improperly.

Tip: Be sure to check for fingerprints that tend to accumulate on doors and cupboards, especially along the top rim. These can be easy for you to overlook, but may be the first thing your customer sees when she enters her bathroom. It's keeping up with details like these that give your work a real finished look.

At this point all the surfaces in the bathroom have been cleaned and rinsed, and should still be damp. Now you can go on to the glasswork. I like to call this process "shining," and the sparkling results are the mark of a true professional. Begin by thoroughly spraying the mirrors with glass cleaner. Then wipe them down using a dry cloth, or preferably a paper towel. Starting at the top wipe toward the bottom. Then rewipe the area using a circular motion. Turn your cloth several times during this procedure, making sure that no streaks or water spots are left behind. Don't overlook trouble spots, like the sides of the medicine chests which are often marked with fingerprints, and the place where the mirror meets the counter- top. Pay careful attention to the mirrors and they will be a perfect reflection of your good work.

Next use your glass cleaner to spray the chrome in the shower and polish it to a sheen with your dry cloth. Go on to spray the other surfaces you've already cleaned, the shower doors, the entire toilet area and the countertops, wiping each section dry as you spray. Make certain that no film is left behind, and when you are finished everything will sparkle.

Tip: When going through this "shining process" it is not necessary to dry the entire shower and tub area. You only need to shine the outside, which the eye sees immediately. You can allow the inside to dry itself naturally. I usually spray the outside and top of the clean tub with glass cleaner and shine it until it gleams.

Now that the entire bathroom is clean (except for the floor, which will be cleaned later) it is time to replace all the knick knacks and toiletry items that you removed earlier. If you were careful to place the items on the floor in the right order when you removed them, it should be easy now to return them where they belong. As you pick up each item to replace it wipe it down to remove dust and sticky fingerprints, but don't do this over any of the surfaces you just cleaned, or you will have to wipe them down all over again. Think ahead and you will save yourself a lot of extra work.

In the shower area put back the razors, bottles and soaps, wiping everything thoroughly so they are not sticky. Make sure there is no hair stuck to the soap. This is a small point easily overlooked, but it makes a big difference. Make sure that all the objects in the bathroom have been wiped down, including tissue boxes, hair brush handles, curling irons, dixie cup dispensers and toilet paper roll holders. Picture frames get dusty in bathrooms, and so do towel racks. After you've emptied the bathroom trash into the bag you brought for that purpose, wipe out the trash basket so it shines and doesn't have any sticky lotion drips or powder in it.

Since we still have to clean the bathroom floor, place the trash can, scales, and all other items that are on the floor onto the carpeting. This is the time to gently shake the rugs and mats onto the unvacuumed carpeting. All the rugs and mats in the kitchen, entry way and other areas should be gently shaken onto the unvacuumed carpeting before going on to the next step.

Before you leave the bathroom turn and look at it carefully. Are the towels folded neatly? Is everything off the floor? Did you wipe all the fingerprints off of the medicine chests and the door handle? Is the mirror free of streaks and spots? If you are satisfied, go on to do the next bathroom in the same way. When all the bathrooms have been cleaned and shined in the same manner, you are ready to go on to the dusting.

Summary Of Bathroom Cleaning Procedure.

1. *Open windows for ventilation.*
2. *Put bowl cleaner in toilet.*
3. *Remove all objects from countertops and shower area.*
4. *Fill sink with disinfectant cleaner and dilute with water.*
5. *Clean and rinse shower area, toilet, countertops and sink, in that order.*
6. *Clean mirror with glass cleaner, and shine rest of bathroom.*

7. *Return all objects to countertops and shower area, wiping each item as it is replaced.*
8. *Wipe out trash can. Wipe down towel racks. Replace towels neatly.*
9. *Remove trash can, mats, rugs, etc. and place on a carpeted area.*
10. *Check your work. How does the bathroom look?*

DUSTING AND GLASSWORK

Remember that in our general plan for cleaning the house we will be moving toward the kitchen, which will be the last room cleaned. Therefore, you should start dusting in the room farthest from the kitchen. If it is a two-story house you will begin upstairs in the most remote room. As you go you can gather dirty glasses that might have been left in the rooms so you can eventually take them to the kitchen. It's a good idea to take dirty glasses and dishes or other items to be moved and place them outside of the door of the room where you are working until you are finished in that room. If you don't take care of this as soon as you see each object you're apt to forget them. Then you will have to waste time later, making a special trip back to retrieve them.

To get yourself ready to dust, move your cleaning bucket with all the supplies to the kitchen where it will be out of the way, waiting for you when you need it later. For now just take with you your dusting rags and your polish (for coffee tables, wooden dressers, etc.). Later you will need your glass cleaner (for television screens, glass tables, plastics, the glass in picture frames, etc.) The method I prefer is to dust first throughout the house, returning later to put the final shine on the glass in each room. Take your rags and polish and go to the room where you will be working first.

There are two important things to remember about dusting that will save you a lot of extra work later.

1. *If you are using a spray furniture polish, always spray the polish onto the rag itself, and never directly onto the piece of furniture you are polishing. The reason for this is to avoid accidentally spraying the polish onto walls, knick knacks and lamps, which would then need to be cleaned (assuming the oil stains would come out at all). To avoid this simply spray your cloth in an open area away from the piece you want to polish. Now you can just dust the furniture with your treated cloth. As you go remove knick knacks and objects from the furniture and then replace immediately, or if you prefer, completely remove the objects by setting them on the floor, dust the area, and then replace.*
2. *Never dust knick knacks with the same cloth you're using to apply polish. Knick knacks usually fall into the glasswork category and will be cleaned later with the glass cleaner. You don't want to gum them up with furniture polish first.*

It is good to keep in mind that furniture polish goes a long way, and it is better to use too little than too much. Also, when you dust make sure you do a thorough job. Don't overlook legs of chairs, headboards, picture frames, window sills, and the sides of furniture, which can also collect dust and fingerprints. When dusting remember to always work from the top down, or you'll find yourself doing the same area over and over.

Be aware that each client may have her own preferred method for cleaning her home. Her mother may have done things a certain way, and now she feels that unless she uses the same method her house is not really clean, or that she may be hurting her furniture. One woman may prefer that you not use any polish at all. Another woman may want you to dust using her vacuum cleaner attachments. These attachments do work well on lamp shades, wicker and other hard-to-clean areas. Find out how each of your clients wants things done and what equipment might be available to you. Then cooperate with these preferences.

Once every room has been completely dusted, you are ready to go back to the first room and begin the glasswork. Take with you your glass cleaner and a clean, dry rag or paper towel. Spray the cleaner onto your cloth, using the same technique you used for your polish, and dust pictures and frames, television screens, knick knacks, and so on. You will clean everything made of glass or plastic in this way, including telephones, ash trays, vases, chrome chairs, lamps and glass tables. Most likely, anything you didn't use polish on earlier, you will now be shining with the glass cleaner. You will probably need to spray the glass cleaner directly onto any mirrors, but be careful not to spray any on the walls or other surfaces.

The best way to clean a glass table is to take everything off of it before you begin. It may seem easier at first to simply wipe around the objects sitting on top, but you will end up making it harder on yourself the next time you clean. Also, imagine what your client will think when she picks up her ash tray, only to find a big smudge under it.

Straighten up magazines and other loose items as you go so that everything will have an overall neat appearance. Now turn around and check the room before you leave. Have you dusted everything, leaving no streaks or fingerprints? Is all the glass and chrome shining? Have you removed all the dirty glasses and things to take to the kitchen? Have you emptied the trash? If so, move on to the next room.

When you've dusted and then shined the whole house in this way, you are ready to begin work in the kitchen.

Summary Of Dusting And Glasswork.

1. *Start in the room farthest from the kitchen.*
2. *Treat your dust cloth with polish and dust furniture throughout the house.*
3. *Treat your cloth with glass cleaner and do the glasswork throughout the house.*
4. *Remove dirty glasses, etc.*
5. *Straighten up magazines, etc. so everything is neat.*
6. *Check your work. How does the room look?*

CLEANING THE KITCHEN

In the kitchen a little pre-planning and organization is very important. If you will have a major job to do in this room, such as cleaning the inside of the oven or the refrigerator, you will want to attend to that first. Specific instructions for cleaning the oven appear at the end of this chapter. But that, and cleaning the inside of the refrigerator, are special jobs that you will not be concerned with normally, so for now let's concentrate on the usual procedure for general kitchen cleaning.

We will approach the kitchen in the same way we did the bathrooms, making sure first of all that the area is well ventilated. To begin, clear all surfaces to be cleaned of objects and appliances. You could move these objects from one side of the counter to the other as you clean, or better still, get them out of the way by placing them on the floor. This is fine because you will be wiping off all these objects thoroughly before replacing them. Try to put things on the floor in the order that you removed them from the counters so that you can replace them in their original spots. Now you are ready to prepare your disinfectant cleaning solution in the sink (just as you did in the bathroom.)

When your solution is prepared, you are ready to begin cleaning. Start with the countertops, using the sink as a divider. Start cleaning from one outside end of the counter, moving the dirt toward the sink. Then do the same thing starting from the opposite end. Clean thoroughly, wiping the sides of the counter and the ledges where the counter meets the wall. Check for spots on the wall above the counter. When you are satisfied that all is clean move on to the stove. Do not clean the sink at this point. You will be continuing to use the cleaning solution that you have prepared in it as you do the rest of the kitchen.

The stove is usually the hardest part of the kitchen

to clean. Stove tops are often not cleaned properly after each use, and therefore have a build-up of grease and baked-on food. You may have to take extra measures to clean the stove thoroughly, such as concentrating your cleaning solution or using a mild abrasive. Be careful though that you don't scratch the surface.

When cleaning the stove you will do a better job if you can remove the burners, rings and metal drip trays. On some of the newer models many parts of the stove are removable, including the knobs. Just make sure you watch to see how everything goes so you can put it back correctly. No matter what, never force anything! You don't want to have to pay to replace broken parts, nor do you want to inconvenience your client.

Now that the stove and countertops are done, clean the remaining kitchen surfaces with your disinfectant cleaning solution. This includes the outsides of the dishwasher, trash compactor, etc. Start with the appliances farthest from the sink and work your way in. Take special care to do a good job on the refrigerator. This is one area that always gets noticed. Don't forget the top. You may not be able to see what's going on up there, but your client's 6'4" husband will! Do an extra careful job on the door handles. The refrigerator door handle is the primary collector of jelly, cookie batter and other sticky substances which will hide from you on the side of the handle you cannot see. But that is the first thing your client will feel when she comes home and reaches for a cold drink. Don't let the dirty door handle be your downfall! Clean every part of it well.

When all the surfaces have been wiped with the disinfectant cleaner you can rinse them down. Make sure everything is squeaky clean, getting off all the soapy residue and grit. When you are satisfied that all is clean, it is time to give the kitchen that professional shine. For this you will need your glass cleaner again.

Spray the counters with the glass cleaner and wipe dry with a dry cloth or paper towel. Do extra detail work in the area above the sink, making sure the soap dishes are gleaming. The chrome around the faucet should be given special attention. When the chrome has a mirror-like shine the whole kitchen looks fresh and clean, so rub everything carefully and thoroughly, leaving it with a bright shine and no streaks. Go on to shine the other surfaces you've already cleaned, being sure not to miss the kitchen table.

Now that the countertops have been cleaned and shined you can replace all the small appliances and knick knacks you removed earlier. Try to put everything back in its proper place. As you replace each item wipe it down. This includes blenders, can openers, toaster ovens, flower vases, etc. Wipe all the surfaces, including the bottom, and take special care to shine the chrome so that it has that professional gleam. If an appliance is especially dirty, such as a can opener encrusted with tomato sauce, you will have to put down your glass cleaner and touch up the item with the cleaning solution that is still sitting in the sink. Except for mirrors and glass, your glass cleaner is for shining only, not cleaning. Learn to use your different products appropriately and you will get the best results while conserving your energy.

Now you are ready for the final step, cleaning the sink. To do this properly you will probably need to use an abrasive cleaner. Drain the sink of the cleaning solution you've been using and apply the abrasive. If the sink is especially stained you may need to apply the abrasive ahead of time, possibly when you first enter the kitchen. If your client has a double sink and one side is stained you can sprinkle the abrasive on the stains and use the other side to prepare your cleaning solution. If there is only a single sink, or both sides of a double sink are stained badly, you may want to prepare your cleaning solution in your bucket so that you can pre-treat the sink. As you become more familiar with the cleaning process you will learn to notice little things like a stained sink the moment you enter the room. Then, with a little pre-planning, you can reduce the amount of elbow grease you'll have to use later on.

Sometimes a client may request that you do a special job such as cleaning the inside of an oven or refrigerator, or oiling her cupboards. Think about what you will need to do to accomplish these jobs, and plan your time accordingly. A little thought can save you from spending four hours cleaning a house, when you could have done it in two.

When you think the kitchen is done take one final look. Is everything shining? No fingerprints or streaks? Is everything dusted? Did you take care of the trash? Are all rugs and mats off the kitchen floor? When you are certain that the kitchen is clean you are ready to move on to the final step, cleaning and vacuuming the floors, so put away all your supplies except those you still need (bucket, mop, broom, floor cleaner and/or polish).

Summary Of Kitchen Cleaning Procedure.

1. *Make sure room is well-ventilated.*
2. *Remove all objects from surfaces to be cleaned.*
3. *Fill sink with disinfectant cleaner diluted with water.*
4. *Clean and rinse stove, countertops, refrigerator and other surfaces.*
5. *Shine all surfaces with glass cleaner.*
6. *Return all objects to countertops, wiping each as it is replaced.*
7. *Clean and shine sink.*
8. *Check your work. How does the room look?*

CLEANING AND VACUUMING THE FLOORS

You are now ready for the final stage of cleaning the house, cleaning and vacuuming the floors. You will start by cleaning all the bare floors. Then the final vacuuming will put the finishing touch on your work.

Cleaning The Bare Floors.

You will usually find bare floors in the entryway, bathroom and kitchen. These uncarpeted floors may be made of linoleum, wood or tile. Cleaning this kind of floor is easy if you have first picked up all the dust, lint and other foreign matter that may have accumulated on it. If you wet the floor while it still has clumps of dust on it, you will make a mess. Therefore the first step to cleaning a bare floor is to prepare it by sweeping or vacuuming it. To begin, make sure all the mats, rugs, trash etc. have been removed. Now you are ready to pick up the dust. You can sweep the floor using a broom and dust pan if necessary. However, if your client's vacuum has a special attachment for hard floors by all means use it. A vacuum is much more effective at removing dirt than a broom, and it can save you time.

Do check with your client ahead of time about how certain surfaces should be treated. For example, she may not want you to wash a hardwood floor at all. With linoleum or tile there is usually no problem.

Assuming that you have determined which floors you will and will not wash, you must start by first preparing your cleaning solution. You will not want to have to dirty one of your carefully cleaned sinks, so make sure ahead of time that your client can provide you with a bucket. Let me note here that it wouldn't be a bad idea for you to carry some basic supplies (like a bucket) with you in your car. While it is true that at the time you first meet your client to estimate her house you will tell her that she must provide all necessary supplies, you cannot be certain that she will remember to do so. It never hurts to come prepared for an emergency. It will save you a lot of time, and you can gently remind her later of what she has forgotten.

Getting back to cleaning the bare floors, take your bucket with the cleaning solution to the most remote room in the house you will have to clean this way. In a two-story house, start upstairs. Following the directions on the cleaner you are using, proceed to clean the floor.

It is a matter of personal preference whether you

use a long-handled mop or wash the floor on your hands and knees. I find that if the floor only covers a small area it is best to clean it on your hands and knees, especially if it is the first time you are cleaning that house. Washing a floor this way enables you to clean into all the corners and crevices that a mop simply cannot reach. You can get at all those funny little places where dirt accumulates. The result is a floor with a better overall look. This method is also much faster. You don't have to get out a mop and prepare a bucket, and you don't have to worry about splashing water up onto walls or surfaces you've just finished cleaning. If your knees bother you, you can pick up an inexpensive pair of knee pads. If you have a large area to clean you may prefer to use a mop, but check the corners and other odd places that may need special attention.

Here is an important floor-cleaning tip that will save you from unnecessary extra work. Your client may request that you use the type of floor cleaner that you apply directly onto the floor from the bottle. If so you want to make sure that you hold the bottle close to the floor as you squirt out the product to avoid splattering. Splattered wax on sliding glass doors and walls can leave unattractive stains that are very difficult to remove. You can save yourself the frustration of having to stop your work to clean up the mess by being careful to avoid the problem in the first place. I recommend that you hold the bottle only an inch or two from the floor as you pour.

Finally, here is something to consider if you use a mop to clean the floor. Years of experience have taught me that cleaning a floor with a mop tends to leave streaks, no matter how careful you are. I have discovered a technique, however, that really helps. I place a rag between the mop and the floor as follows. Dampen a rag or dishtowel (about one foot square) in your cleaning solution, wring it out, and place it on the floor. Lay the mop head in the center of the rag and wrap the corners up around the mop. Now mop as usual, stopping occasionally to rinse out the rag. This has the same effect as washing the floor on your knees, only it's easier because you're guiding the rag with your long-handled mop while standing up. And best of all, this eliminates streaks, leaving the floor with a nice, even shine.

Now that all the bare floors are clean you are ready to vacuum. As you go back through the house to vacuum you can replace the rugs and other objects you had removed in order to wash the floors. By this time the floors you did first should be dry.

Vacuuming.

We now come to the final step in the cleaning process: vacuuming. Vacuuming adds immeasurably to the overall look of a professionally cleaned house. A properly vacuumed carpet gives dimension to a house, just as freshly patted pillows give dimension to a couch. The whole room looks "fluffed up" when the nap on the carpet has been brushed and raised, bringing out its rich color and texture. It is important that you learn the correct technique for vacuuming so that the full beauty of the carpet is brought out and your work throughout the house is shown to its best advantage.

This may sound funny, but the most important aspect of vacuuming technique that you will have to master is learning what to do with the cord. There are two points about this that you need to understand. First, you always want to make sure that the vacuum cord is plugged into a socket which is behind you. The reason for this is that you never want to have to walk over a carpet that you have just vacuumed. Your footprints going across the rug will ruin the effect you have worked so hard to achieve. We have saved the vacuuming for last so there will be no reason to walk back over the rugs, and that includes going back to unplug the vacuum.

The second point is that you will have to examine the house and work in it to discover the arrangement of sockets and decide how best to use them. It can be very annoying to be constantly stepping over and around the cord or having to loosen the cord from where it has gotten caught on pieces of furniture. It can be even more annoying to have to stop your work in order to replug the cord into a new socket because you've run out of length. Instead of getting frustrated when difficulties arise, simply find a better place to plug in the cord. Sometimes a vacuum will come with a very short cord, which means you could waste a lot of time unplugging and replugging it. I suggest you bring your own extension cord in that situation. A good, long extension cord can really make the vacuuming go fast.

Your client may have a vacuum with a variety of attachments. These can be very handy for cleaning baseboards, lamp shades and difficult to reach places. If such a machine is available you will find it easier to use these attachments first, perhaps when you first take out the vacuum to remove the dust from the bare floors. Do the final vacuuming last.

Begin your final vacuuming in the most distant corner of the house. In a two-story house you will begin upstairs with the cord plugged in behind you, vacuum backwards. Try to raise the nap on the carpet evenly, leaving as few marks as possible from the vacuum cleaner itself. This may be difficult with some machines, but with time you can learn how to handle any machine more effectively. If you are cleaning a two-story house be sure to vacuum the steps. Once you have completed vacuuming the second floor you should have no reason to have to go upstairs again.

Now you can follow the same procedure to do the bottom floor. By the time you have finished vacuuming the downstairs, the whole house will look and smell terrific, and you will have that wonderful sense of satisfaction that comes from doing a job well. Look around the house as you leave and think how pleased your customer will be when she comes home and sees your work.

SPECIAL JOBS

Occasionally your client may request that you do a special job that is not part of the basic cleaning process we have just discussed. You should always charge extra for these jobs which you did not include in the estimate you gave on first seeing the house.

Plan your time carefully so your entire schedule isn't upset by a special job. If a certain cleaning product you'll be using needs to sit for a certain length of time, apply it early so it will be ready for the next step when you are. Always plan to do a major job first. If you will be cleaning the oven, do it before you clean the rest of the kitchen. If you don't, you will find yourself cleaning the kitchen a second time.

Here are instructions for some special jobs you may occasionally be asked to do.

Cleaning The Inside Of The Oven

If you are going to clean the inside of an oven, the first thing you must determine is whether or not it is a self-cleaning appliance. If you use an oven cleaning product in a self-cleaning oven you could possibly damage it permanently. It would probably be best to ask your client how she normally cleans her oven, or if there is anything about it you need to know. Being a little cautious at the beginning can protect you from any difficulties later.

Read the directions on your oven cleaner carefully so that you can schedule your time properly. You may discover that in order to work effectively the product needs to sit in a pre-heated oven for twenty minutes. In that case you would want to take a few minutes to apply the oven cleaner early, maybe before you dust. If the oven is especially dirty you may want to apply the product as soon as you arrive at the house so that it will have maximum time to work. The more time the product has to work, the less time you will need to work and the less energy you will need to expend.

The directions on most oven cleaning products recommend that you spread newspapers on the floor around the stove and then spray on the product inside the oven. Be sure to spray the racks too, just as you spray the rest of the oven, and then let them sit in the oven while you go about your work elsewhere.

When you are ready to clean the oven, remove the racks and place them by the sink. You will be doing the racks first so that your cleaning product will have more time to work on the interior of the oven. Fill the sink with water and add whatever other cleaner you wish, making sure it is compatible with the oven cleaner. You will probably need to use some kind of abrasive pad or powder in order to completely remove all the baked-on residue. When the racks are thoroughly cleaned you are ready to proceed to the inside of the oven.

When cleaning the oven you certainly don't want to have to do anything more than once, so remember our rule of thumb that has been so helpful throughout the house: always work from the top down. To clean the oven most efficiently start with the top of the interior. Then do the back panel, working down toward the bottom. Then do each side panel, working from top down. Always finish each panel completely before moving on to the next. Finally, clean the bottom. Rinse the entire oven thoroughly and then dry. Clean the oven door last.

Tip: If the oven light has been on and the bulb is hot, do not touch it. If you touch a hot bulb with your cool, wet cloth, the change in temperature could easily cause it to explode. Turn the light off and let it cool down before you wipe off anything inside the oven.

Windows

Cleaning windows on the inside is an easy job, although it can take up a lot of time. Just spray your glass cleaner all over the window and wipe with a clean cloth or paper towel (just as you cleaned the mirrors in the bathroom).

If the outsides of the windows are easy to reach, your client might want you to do them as well. They will probably be pretty dirty and you need to get that layer of dirt off first. Wash the window with a sponge or rag and water until all the gritty dirt is removed. Then use your glass cleaner to shine the windows, taking special care not to leave any streaks.

Oiling The Cabinets

Oiling kitchen cabinets can be very time-consuming, but the results can brighten up the whole kitchen. There are several products you can use that are very effective. Liquid furniture polish, available in most grocery stores, can bring out the shine on even the dingiest cabinets. You can use one of these products if the cabinets are real wood and are not too greasy. Special wood soaps, also available in most stores, make wonderful wood cleaners, and work well on cabinets that are especially sticky and need a good scrubbing. If your client has a certain product she wants you to use, use it.

If the cabinets are not made of wood, you can clean them easily with dishwashing soap and water.

These special jobs all take up a good deal of extra time, so charge for your work, and plan your schedule accordingly.

SUMMARY AND CONCLUSION

In this chapter I have outlined a system of cleaning that will enable you to clean any house effectively and efficiently. I know this system works because I've used it myself hundreds of times, and I've taught it to others who have gone on to become excellent professional housecleaners themselves. You and your client both want you to do as good a job as possible. You want to use your precious time and energy as efficiently as possible. This system lets you do both.

Here is a quick review of the system of cleaning that will change your cleaning routine forever.

The two basic rules that you will follow are:

1. Always work from the top down.
2. Always do like jobs at the same time.

The order in which you perform in a house:

1. Clean all bathrooms (except for floors)
2. Dust
3. Do glasswork
4. Clean kitchen (except for floor)
5. Do all bare floors
6. Vacuum the carpets

Once you've adapted this routine to a particular house, stick with it. This efficient method lets you clean a house in the least time while still attending to all the details.

Follow the procedure outlined here and you will find yourself enjoying a job that lets you earn excellent money and gives you a great feeling of satisfaction. There is something very nice and satisfying about a house that is fresh and clean. There is also something very nice and satisfying about knowing that you have given your customer the best job possible for her money. The cleaning system described here gives you the means to accomplish both. Once you've tried the system yourself, you'll see how fast and easy cleaning a house really is – and you'll make great money doing it!

CHAPTER SIX

How to Estimate a House

IF you've studied the previous chapter you're now an expert on how to clean a house like a professional. You're ready to go over to Mrs. A's house to give her an estimate of how much you would charge to clean her house on a regular basis. At this point it is very important that you make a good impression. You must convince Mrs. A that you're knowledgeable about the cleaning business, reliable and willing to work hard. Mrs. A will be entrusting her precious possessions to you and she needs to feel that her decision to hire you is one that she will be happy with.

As soon as Mrs. A opens the door to greet you your appearance will make an impression on her, so when you plan what to wear remember all those rules we discussed earlier. Wear something neat, clean and comfortable that makes you look like a housecleaner. The sweats and a t-shirt that you would normally be working in would be fine. If you look like you just came from cleaning another house, all the better. With your hair pulled back, simple makeup, little or no jewelry and plain, unpolished fingernails, you'll look perfect for the part. Your enthusiasm for your work will be much more attractive to Mrs. A than a designer wardrobe. The worst thing you can do is to make her feel that you are competing with her or threatening her in any way. If that happens, you won't get the job. So just remember what you're there for, and dress accordingly.

LOCATING THE HOUSE

The day for your interview with Mrs. A has arrived. Before you set out and drive all the way over to her house, I would suggest that you call her to confirm that you are on your way. You can just be bright and cheery and say something like: "Hello, Mrs. A. This is Mary, the housecleaner. I just wanted to let you know that I'm on my way to meet you for our 3:00 appointment." There are two reasons why you want to do this. First, it is a very professional thing to do and Mrs. A will appreciate your courtesy. Second, it could save you a lot of time and trouble if you get the following response. "Oh, Mary, I'm so glad you called. I looked all over for your phone number and couldn't find it. I just remembered that I have to go pick up my husband at the airport and won't be able to see you today. Can we reschedule for tomorrow?" You would be amazed at how often this kind of thing happens, and it can be very frustrating to go over to a house all eager and enthusiastic only to find that nobody is home. It's far better to check ahead of time. If a client cancels when you call, don't let her know you're annoyed. Every house is important, so just tell her that you understand and would be happy to reschedule the appointment. Then make sure she has your name and number so that she can call you in case anything else comes up.

Assuming that you have confirmed your appointment, you are now ready to go over to the house. Plan to leave your home pretty early for this first visit. You might have trouble finding the house or something else could come up and you don't want to risk being late. Be sure you have the index card you made up on your client with you, with her name and address and directions for reaching her house. It is also a good idea to bring a map with you, especially if you are unfamiliar with the area and the streets are rather complicated.

If you know several days in advance that you'll be visiting a certain house you could even drive by and look for it ahead of time, just so you'll know exactly where it is. You'll have enough on your mind when you go to give the estimate without having to worry about getting lost. Of course it isn't necessary that you drive by in advance, especially if you know the neighborhood well. Just keep it in mind as something you might want to do under certain circumstances.

But let's say you're on the way to the house, following the directions on your index card, and for some reason you still can't find it. Who knows, maybe Mrs. A gave you the wrong turn, or you wrote it down wrong. The next thing to do is to look around to see if anyone is walking down the street who might be able to help you. If no one is around, or no one can tell you where the street is, then simply drive to the nearest public phone and call your client. Fortunately you have your index card with her phone number on it (see how important that card is), and since you left your house early, you're still not late. Just tell your client that you've driven around looking for the house but can't find it. Ask her to give you the directions again. If you read back to her the directions you've written on your card she can probably tell you right away where the mistake was made. When you're sure of how to get there thank her and tell her you'll see her in a few minutes. Usually you won't have to go through all this because you'll have no trouble finding the house. But if you ever do get lost, there is no need to panic. Just call the client. As long as you leave your house with plenty of time to spare and you have that all-important index card with you, everything is alright.

Once you find the house, the next step is to park the car. Even a small thing like this can mark you as a professional, or cause you to seem inconsiderate. No matter how tight the parking situation is, do not park in the driveway. For one thing, you don't know if someone will be pulling up soon or may need to leave in a hurry. But even more important, your car could easily leak oil. Your client won't be favorably impressed if you leave a big, unsightly oil stain in the middle of her brand new driveway.

When you've parked your car in a trouble-free area, walk up to the door and knock. Say to whoever answers, "Hello, I'm Mary, the housecleaner. I'm here to give you an estimate for cleaning your house." Be pleasant and polite so that everyone feels comfortable.

At this point most people will ask you, "What do you want me to show you first?" The best thing to say is, "Why don't you just show me through the house and tell me exactly what you would like to have done."

Before we go through the house, however, I want to make another important point about going to the interview. It would be best if you could go to the interview alone. Of course there may be circumstances that will make you feel uncomfortable to go alone. Perhaps you will be going to the home of a single man and you'd like to meet him with someone else the first time. However, in most cases you should go alone. If you don't have your own transportation and need someone to drive you, ask your driver if they wouldn't mind waiting in the car for you. Warn them ahead of time that the estimate could take up to half an hour so they can bring something to read if they want. You want to meet the client alone so that she will see you're confident and independent. Also, you don't want her to wonder if you'll be bringing strangers to her house while you're working there. All these little things add to your client's good impression of you, and you will benefit in the end.

HOW TO DECIDE WHAT TO CHARGE

No matter how large or small a house is, it can be divided into different sections, which are then used to determine how much to charge. Since you already know the cleaning process, this will be easy for you to do. These are the questions you will ask yourself as Mrs. A shows you through her home:

1. *How many bathrooms are there?*
    a. *How much glasswork is there in the bath rooms?*
    b. *Is there a tub or shower in the bathroom? (These take the most time.)*
2. *How many bedrooms?*
3. *How much dusting and glasswork is there?*
4. *How large is the kitchen area? Are there many appliances? Will it take a long time?*
5. *How many bare floors and how big are they?*
6. *How much vacuuming?*

To determine how much you will charge for a particular house, you must first determine what you will charge to do an "average" house. Now first of all, you know about how much money you'd like to make. Second, it's very helpful to call other housecleaners who advertise in the paper and ask them how much they charge. After you talk to several people you'll get a feel for what the going rate is in your area.

Some people charge by the hour, but I don't recommend this. It doesn't give you any flexibility with your time, and you have no incentive to work straight through the house and be done quickly. A good housecleaner should take less time to finish a house once she's done it a few times, and she shouldn't have to hold herself back so she can fill her time. You'll find yourself making much more money getting paid by the job than by the hour.

Getting back to determining a price for cleaning a particular house, let's assume the average house will cost $40 to clean. This $40 covers the basic cleaning process we've already described in the last chapter, and does not include any of the extras. The basic cleaning process includes cleaning the bathrooms, dusting, glasswork, cleaning the kitchen, washing the bare floors and vacuuming. It does not include things like cleaning the inside of appliances, waxing floors or washing windows.

Let's say Mrs. A has a one-story, 4-bedroom house with 2 bathrooms. The bare floors to be mopped include both bathrooms and an entryway. Average dusting and minimal glasswork are required. So far this is an average house in the $40 range.

But now let's take a look at the extras. Suppose Mrs. A wants you to put clean linens on her bed each time you do her house. She also wants you to clean her sliding glass window every time. Adding these two extras will make it a $45 house.

Do not be hesitant about taking on extras that the customer is willing to pay for. The more money you can get from a house the better, and that extra $5 will add up. Think of it this way. If you become a full-time housecleaner you will do 2 houses a day, or 10 houses each week. This may sound like a lot at first, but don't worry. If you've cleaned a house really well the first time, after that it's a breeze. Some houses will be so clean that at first you'll wonder what it is you're supposed to do. You won't be doing major scrubbing and scraping on your regular houses - just easy surface cleaning.

Now, if you're cleaning 2 houses a day and doing some extra work in each one, that extra $5 per house becomes $10 a day. That's $50 a week, or an extra $200 a month. Your little extra job of washing a window or changing the sheets in each house can add up to the monthly payment on your new car. And don't forget, you'll be finishing your houses so quickly with my system, that even with the little extras you'll be done in record time. So if people want special things done, be happy about it and just charge for your additional work.

EXTRA JOBS

Let's look at some of the extra things your client might want to have done. Some of these will be jobs you'll do each time you come to the house and you will charge for them every time. Others are occasional jobs (like cleaning the inside of the oven), and you will add them to the bill only when you do them. The more time it takes for you to do an extra job, the more you should charge for it. Once again, keep in mind that these extra jobs mean more money for you, so don't be afraid to take them on.

Windows

Many customers will ask you if you do windows. Windows are easy to do, but they can be time-consuming. If you were to do all the windows in the house at one time, it would require a special visit and maybe take all day. It's a good idea to suggest to the client that you could simply do one or two windows every time you come to the house, adding maybe $5 to the bill on a regular basis to cover this. Now the windows will be clean all the time, and the cost to the client will be kept down.

Laundry

Laundry is very easy to do but it can take up a lot of time. You must figure that washing, drying and folding one load of laundry covers a 2 hour block of time. Since your average house will only take about 2-3 hours to clean (after you've cleaned it really well a couple of times) I recommend that you agree to do no more than one load per visit. If you have a larger house that takes longer to clean and that brings you $50-$75, you might consider doing 2 loads. If you will be doing laundry you must plan your time well, or you'll end up wasting a lot of time in the house waiting for the laundry to dry. Just remember to put the laundry in the machine as soon as you enter the house. Also, keep track of your time so that you can transfer the laundry from the washer to the dryer as soon as the washer stops.

Ironing

Ironing is a very time-consuming job, that I personally do not enjoy. I recommend that you say no to this, unless it's something you really like to do. It wouldn't be a bad idea to have handy the name and number of someone you know who is willing to iron so you can refer them to your client.

Mini-Blinds

Cleaning mini-blinds is an entire job in itself, and it can be a little tricky. They are better done by a specialist. Here again, if you don't want to tackle this job yourself, have the name of someone you can refer to your client.

Wooden Shades

These also take a lot of time to clean, but it is an easy job. Some people have these shades throughout the house and I recommend you do them on a rotating basis, just as you would the windows, adding an extra cost to the bill for each visit. This way the cost to your client will be kept within reason, and you will be able to keep down the amount of time you have to spend in the house.

Polishing Silver

Polishing silver is an easy, pleasant job, but it does take time. If you agree to do this read the directions on the silver cleaner carefully, and wear gloves to protect your hands.

It can take up to half an hour to polish a 5-piece tea set, so don't agree to do more than that if you are only going to charge $7.50 for the service.

Washing and Oiling Kitchen Cupboards

This will take about 20 minutes to do, so it is also about a $7.50 job. Work this job into your regular cleaning schedule. See the section on this under "Special Jobs" in the chapter on "The Cleaning Process."

Dishes

It doesn't take much time to put dishes into a dishwasher if there aren't too many of them and there is space in the machine. If the client leaves out pots and pans that need a lot of work, and you haven't made arrangements to be paid extra to do the dishes, I would just rinse them off and leave them on the side, or actually set them in the sink.

If you start washing dishes without charging for the service, you may find yourself doing a load of dishes every time you come to the house, and you won't like that.

DETERMINING A BASE RATE

Now that we know what the basic housecleaning includes, and we've looked at some of the extras, we can look at how to figure the regular cost for cleaning a particular house.

First of all, always start out with your base rate for an average house in mind. We will assume that you've done some calling around and have determined that $35 is the going, average rate. This covers the basic cleaning process with no extras. Now you will have to look at each house individually to see if this $35 rate for basic cleaning is too high, too low or just right. You might want to charge less for a smaller house, and more for a larger house. But you can't go by size alone. You have to go by the amount of work each house will require just to do the basic cleaning. Sometimes a smaller-sized house will require more and will take more time than a larger one.

Let's say the house is a small, one-story model, but it has a large number of glass tables and mirrors and there's a great deal of dusting to be done. The client has many knick knacks that she wants removed from the shelves and dusted carefully. Then she wants you to use all the attachments on her vacuum to clean the baseboards and odd corners. Even though this is a small house with only one bedroom and bath, it could easily be a $35-

$40 job.

On the other hand you might have a two-story house with 4 bedrooms and 3 baths. Your clients are a married couple with no children. They only use 2 of the bathrooms, and use the shower in only one of these. Therefore, even though there are 3 bathrooms you'll only be cleaning two, and one will take no time at all because you won't have to clean a shower or bathtub, which is the most time-consuming job. Looking at the rest of the house, there are no glass tables and very little other glasswork to be done. Your client tells you that it's alright to simply dust around the objects on the tables because it would be too much to move them all. You're happy to hear this because it means the dusting will not take much time at all. There are no bare floors to mop because the bathrooms are carpeted and the kitchen floor is covered with indoor-outdoor carpeting. There are no children living at home and the husband and wife both work, so things don't get too messy during the day. Also, the couple eats out quite a bit so the kitchen is fairly simple to clean. Given all of these facts, you can see that this larger, two-story house could actually take less time to clean than the smaller house described earlier. They are both $35-$40 houses.

The important thing for you to remember is that in setting the base rate for the house it's not enough to just look at the size of the house. You have to look at the details to determine whether you need to go above or below the average rate.

ADDING ON THE EXTRAS

Let's say you've determined a house to be a $35 job for the basic cleaning. Now you have to add the extras. As a rule of thumb, charge about $7.50 for extra jobs that will take about 20 minutes to half an hour. Charge about $15 if you'll have to spend an additional hour in the house doing extras. For example, if you'll be cleaning 2 windows per visit (about 15 minutes) and changing the linens on 2 beds (another 15 minutes), this will bring your $35 house closer to $45. If the client also wants you to remove everything from her liquor cabinet, polish it and wash and shine all the glasses in it individually (20 minutes), this will now bring the cost to clean the house up to around $50. If the client thinks this is too high, don't be afraid to explain to her that you could clean the house for the base rate of $35, but if she really wants the extras done, you will have to charge her more.

REACHING AN AGREEMENT WITH YOUR CLIENT

There are three things for you to remember at this point. The first is, be careful about agreeing to do something extra "just one time" without being paid for it. Your client will come to expect that extra service, free of charge, every time you clean her house, and she will get upset if you don't do it.

Second, have confidence in your estimate. Of course the client is going to want to pay less, or get as many extras as she can included in the basic rate. She may tell you that her old cleaner did the house for $40, and she doesn't see why you want to charge her $45. But you know how much time it will take to clean her house, and how good a job you'll be doing. You know that $45 is a fair price. Your conversation may go something like this:

Client: Your estimate of $45 seems high. I used to have a woman come in every other week to clean my house for only $40.

You: I understand that you may be able to find someone to clean your house for $40, and if you want to keep looking that's up to you. I just know that for the kind of quality work I do this is a $45 job. I do a very thorough job and I am very reliable and responsible. I guarantee my work. In fact, after I clean your house for the first time I'll ask you to go through it thoroughly and let me know if I missed anything or if you find any kind of problem. I know everyone is different and likes to have things done differently, and I make it a point to be sure that I do everything just the way you like it. You have a beautiful home and I know I would enjoy cleaning it and keeping it looking its best. You will absolutely get your money s worth.

If that doesn't convince her to pay the extra $5, then nothing will!

This brings us to the third point. Sometimes you may find a client who absolutely refuses to pay more than the $40 she's always paid to somebody else. This is where you have to make a decision. You know the house is worth $45, and that's what you want to be paid. If you're already cleaning many houses and you know you can find another house easily you may feel it's not worth it for you to tie yourself up with a house for which you're not getting fully paid. You can just thank the woman for her time, and leave. But let's say you've just started in the business. You don't have many houses and you really need this house. After all, $40 is better than nothing! In that case you may decide to swallow your pride and do the house for $40 for now. At a later date when you're better established you can try to raise your fee for that house, or ask the client to find another cleaner.

RAISING THE RATE ON A HOUSE YOU'VE UNDERESTIMATED

Sometimes in estimating a house you'll make a mistake. You tried to be especially reasonable in your rates because you really needed this house and didn't want to lose it after spending an hour with the client. Or, the house really didn't seem as though it would require that much time to clean, but after working in it 3 or 4 times you realize it's taking you as much time as a $45 house, and you're only getting $40. This isn't a good situation because you'll find yourself feeling resentful every time you go over to that house. You're unhappy because you're not making enough money for your time. You may be doing work below your usual standards to make up for the difference in pay, and now your client is not happy. She doesn't know that you're not satisfied with the money you're making, but she does see that things aren't getting done quite as she would like them. There is only one way to solve this problem, and that is for you to be completely honest with your client. This should be easy for you for two reasons. First, you've already developed a relationship with this woman and can talk with her freely. Second, by this time you probably have quite a few houses to clean and you know you can keep going financially even if you lose this one. You've become an expert at finding new houses, and you can replace this one easily if you have to. You have nothing to lose by explaining to your client that you need more money to clean her house, so speak to her pleasantly and honestly – as a real professional.

You might tell her something like this:

> "Mrs. Smith, I want you to know that I really enjoy cleaning your home, and would like to have you as a client for a long time. But now that I've cleaned the house several times I realize it's taking me longer than I originally thought it would. In order to get fully paid for my time, I really should be getting $45. If you feel it's only worth $40, I'll be happy to continue cleaning the house for that price temporarily until you can find someone else to replace me."

Now who could get upset at that? Your client has no reason to be disturbed by anything you've said. You've been honest with her. You've told her how much you enjoy working for her. You've assured her you won't leave her until she's made other arrangements and that you're not forcing her to pay you more, but giving her the option of finding someone else. In most cases if you have been doing a good job your client will not want to lose you over $5. She'll probably start paying the higher amount right away. If not, you'll easily find a new house where you'll be happier. Whatever happens, you will always find that being honest is the best way to handle a situation like this.

WORKING ON SATURDAYS

Sometimes a client will want you to clean her house on Saturdays. Maybe she works all week, and she wants to be there to watch you when you clean. Perhaps she's uncomfortable about having a stranger enter and work in her house alone. You can hardly blame her. It is difficult to trust people, especially when you don't know anything about them.

From your point of view, however, you're not too keen about working on Saturdays. You want to have the weekend to yourself, just like anyone else. Maybe you want to spend time with your family. On the other hand, you're just starting out in the cleaning business and you need to get houses quickly.

Here is a simple solution. Agree to start off cleaning a house on Saturdays until the client gets to know you, and then switch to a better schedule. To get a new client you can run an ad in the paper with a line like this: "Saturdays also available." Since most housecleaners don't work on Saturday, your ad will really stand out. When the client calls you, tell her: "I'll be happy to clean your house on Saturday a couple of times so that you can get to know me and see what good work I do. Then, if you see that you feel comfortable with me we can schedule your house for a regular time during the week."

This is an excellent way to get houses quickly. In most cases you'll soon be able to arrange a time that is satisfactory to you. You may have to give up a few Saturday mornings or afternoons at first, but before you know it you'll be booked with houses and working a schedule that suits you perfectly.

FINALIZING THE DETAILS

There are certain final details you will have to work out with your client. First, she'll probably want to know how long it will take you to clean her house. You know it will take less time to do the job after you've been working in the house for a while, but your first visit may take much more time. You don't want to be too specific about time anyway, because you don't want her to get the idea that you're working by the hour. Your fee is for the whole job, not the time you spend there. Just be vague and say something like, "It usually takes longer the first time I clean a home. I do most of my houses in about three to four hours, but the actual time depends on what has to be done specifically in each house."

Another question that will come up concerns who will furnish the cleaning supplies. Let the client furnish all supplies and use whatever products she prefers. Tell her, "I find my clients are happier with the results when I use the products they use themselves. That's why I always ask the client to provide all the supplies." Not only will your client be more satisfied, but you'll be saved the expense and bother of purchasing and transporting the supplies yourself. If your client asks you, give her a list of basic supplies you will need in order to do a proper job: a disinfectant cleaner; a toilet bowl cleaner; a glass cleaner; a furniture polish spray (if your client wants you to use one); a bucket; a toilet bowl brush; rags, sponges or paper towels; and a vacuum cleaner.

Now you have to schedule a regular time to clean the house and make arrangements for entering it when no one is home. Make sure the client works out some way to leave a key for you. You don't want to go over to a house, ready to work, and then find you can't get in! Work out a system and then write it down so you won't forget that the key is under the third flower-pot. Which brings us to the final point.

YOUR KEY TO SUCCESS: THE INDEX CARD

You've been talking over many details with your client. There are lots of things you have to remember: don't put polish on the antique desk; clean two windows every week. This is where your trusty index card comes in. You'll never keep track of these details if you don't write them down immediately. So put everything you have to remember on the card, including your cleaning schedule and whatever arrangements you've made to enter the house. Also put down a number where you can reach the client in case something happens while you're in the house.

The index card will remember everything for you. Take it with you when you go to the house. Keep another file copy at home. Learn how to use your index cards and you will always do a professional job, without ever having to worry about forgetting something. Now there will be no surprises for you, or disappointments for your client.

Mrs. Clean $45 every Monday
555-0000 res. 8:00 A.M.
555-1111 bus.

1234 Polish Lane

(Take 95 to Shine Street and make a left. Go to second stop light and make a right on Polish Lane. Second house on right.)

* Appointment for estimate 3:00 Tues. 3/14

Front

General Cleaning:

Don't do kids rooms upstairs.
Don't use any polish on Antique furniture in the living room.
Guest bathroom shower never gets used.

* Key under flower pot on the side of the house

Back

May Schedule

(working only three days a week)

Sunday	Monday	Tuesday	Wednesday	Thursday	Friday	Saturday
	1 Mrs. Smith 8:00 Mrs. Walker 12:00	2	3 Mrs. Williams 8:00 Mrs. Roberts 12:30	4	5 Mrs. Lewis 8:00 Mrs. Stevens 11:30	6
7	8 Mrs. Smith 8:00 Mrs. Walker 12:00	9	10 Mrs. Williams 8:00 Mrs. Roberts 12:30	11	12 Mrs. Lewis 8:00 Mrs. Stevens 11:30	13
14	15 Mrs. Smith 8:00 Mrs. Walker 12:00	16	17 Mrs. Williams 8:00 Mrs. Roberts 12:30	18	19 Mrs. Lewis 8:00 Mrs. Stevens 11:30	20
21	22 Mrs. Smith 8:00 Mrs. Walker 12:00	23	24 Mrs. Williams 8:00 Mrs. Roberts 12:30	25	26 Mrs. Lewis 8:00 Mrs. Stevens 11:30	27
28	29 Mrs. Smith 8:00 Mrs. Walker 12:00	30	31 Mrs. Williams 8:00 Mrs. Roberts 12:30			

Remember, you get to arrange your schedule as you please. You decide which days and hours you want to work.

SUMMARY

Here are the important points you should remember when estimating a house:

1. Dress appropriately and start out early. Don't do things that could leave a bad impression
2. Establish a base rate for cleaning the house, using the amount you want to make to clean an average house (probably $35-$40) as your standard.
3. Add about $7.50 to the cost for each 20 min utes to half an hour spent on extra jobs.
4. Ask the client to furnish all cleaning supplies.
5. Write all the vital facts down on your index card. This includes special instructions from the client and arrangements for entering the house.

CHAPTER SEVEN

The Do's and Don'ts of the Housecleaning Business

HERE are some special tips to keep in mind when you are cleaning someone's home. Most of these points have to do with courtesy and common sense. Be a pleasant worker who does not do things that you would not want a stranger to do in your home, and you will have satisfied clients who will be happy to recommend you to others.

Do Try To Have A Positive Attitude.
When you are in a bad mood your work suffers, and so do the people around you. Whatever is bothering you at home should be left there. Concentrate on your work and you will actually find yourself feeling better as you go.

Don't Argue With Anything Your Client Says.
It is her home, and her money. Use the products and techniques she prefers. You can do what you prefer in your own home.

Do Use The Products Supplied By Your Client.
You may prefer to use another product, but your client will be happier if you use the one she likes. Also, it will cost you money to bring your own supplies.

Don't Offer Suggestions On Products Unless Asked For.

Your client may not want to be corrected by you, and she will not want to go out and invest a lot of money in new supplies. If she asks your opinion you can give it, but don't get insulted if she doesn't follow your advice.

Don't Talk About Someone Else's House.

You may be tempted to talk about how dirty someone else's house is, but don't do it. Your new client may be afraid you'll talk about her house. And, if word gets back to your old client (and it is amazing how fast gossip spreads) you may lose her. Make it a point to always protect your client's privacy.

Do Be On Time.

If you are going to be late, call to let them know. You know how unpleasant it is to have to wait for someone. If you keep a client waiting one too many times, she may decide to find someone more reliable.

Don't Park In Their Driveway.

If your car leaves an unsightly oil leak your clients will not like it. You will not like it if you have to stop your work so they can get their cars in and out of the garage. You can avoid all this trouble by simply parking on the street.

Don't Park In Front Of The Mailbox.

Think ahead about what things might cause any kind of inconvenience, and then avoid them.

Don't Wear Revealing Or Light Clothes.

Wear something that is comfortable for you to work in, and that does not make other people feel uncomfortable to see you in.

Do Leave The Fancy Jewelry And Fingernails At Home.

You want to look like a hard and willing worker who is not afraid to get her hands dirty or her hair a little messed. How can you do a good job if you're worried about breaking a fingernail or getting a bracelet caught on something? Don't wear anything that will slow you down or leave a bad impression.

Don't Bring Anyone With You.

Not a child, husband, friend, anyone. This is the fastest way to lose a house. Your client may trust and like you, but she doesn't want a stranger in her house. And she doesn't want your attention diverted from your work while you entertain your "guest."

Don't Give All Your Friends The Phone Number Where You're Working.

Think how embarrassing it would be if they called when you weren't there. If you must, leave a number where you can be reached in case of an emergency, only give it to someone you trust, and make sure it isn't used unless it really is an emergency.

Don't Smoke In Your Client's House Unless She Tells You It Is Alright.

But don't ever ask if you can or cannot. It is unprofessional. If you must smoke, do it outside. Remember, you are there to clean the house, not add to the mess.

Don't Eat Their Food, Unless They Specifically Tell You And Want You To.

Even then, if you do eat, be conservative. Enjoy their hospitality graciously, but don't look like you're making this the main meal of your day.

Do Read Directions On Products Carefully.

Once you've applied a product incorrectly it is too late. Make sure ahead of time that you are following the correct procedure. Mistakes waste time, and may cost you more than embarrassment.

Don't Put Oily, Dusty Rags On Carpet.

They can cause a stain. Think ahead and avoid a problem later.

Do Check That Your Cleaning Bucket Has A Secure Handle Before You Lift It.

A broken handle on a full bucket will spill dirty water all over the carpet. Need I say more?

Do Be Careful That The Vacuum Cleaner Cord Does Not Get Sucked Up In The Vacuum.

It is amazing how easily this can happen, and it will cost you time and may do serious damage to the cord. While vacuuming always be aware of the location of the cord.

Do Check The Vacuum Cleaner Bags Now And Again.

If they are full or become displaced during operation, the machine will not function properly.

Note: If the vacuum sounds funny there's a good chance that the belt has fallen off or is broken. If you know what you're doing and can fix it easily, do so. But don't do anything that could hurt you or cause further damage.

Do Tell Your People If You Break Something.

Hiding the fact is dishonest, and they will think less of you when they discover the damage themselves. Most people understand that accidents do happen. You will feel better if you report the incident and clear the air.

Do Be Careful That House Pets Don't Get Out If They Are Not Supposed To.

This is a responsibility you will have to face if your client has pets. Just be very aware of yourself as you enter and leave the house.

Do Go Back Through The House Before Leaving To Make Sure Everything Is Done.

For example, did you take out the trash?

Do Turn Out The Lights And Lock The Door Before Leaving.

It is your responsibility to leave the house safe and secure.

As you get more experience cleaning houses you will probably come up with some DO's and DON'TS of your own. This is the time to reflect back and feel a sense of pride for all you've accomplished. Give yourself a pat on the back, you deserve it!

CHAPTER EIGHT

Conclusion

THERE'S a lot of very practical information in this guide. Most of it has been learned from years of personal experience running a housecleaning business and training others to start their own.

I know that the cleaning system described here really can make you very successful at cleaning houses. I also know that anyone who has the desire can use the techniques we've discussed to find and keep clients. But there's only one way that you will ever know this for yourself, and that's to go out and do it.

I know it may seem like a lot at first, but really, once you've tried any of the methods that have been described in such detail here, you'll see just how easy it is. Men and women all over the country are using this program to start their own cleaning businesses and are making excellent money while enjoying flexible hours along with many other benefits. You can too.

Take one step at a time. Try the cleaning system out on your own house and see how well it works. Put an ad in the paper and see what it's like to handle your first call. Little by little your confidence will grow and before you know it, after cleaning a house just one or two times, you'll realize that you truly have developed into a professional.

Take pleasure in the learning process and let the information in this guide be your companion along the way. Good luck!

Rae Ann Luethy

About the Author

RAE ANN Luethy began her own housecleaning business in Southern California at age eighteen. Over the years she has established a successful business and developed a system of cleaning that works in any size or type of home, quickly and efficiently. In 1993, she established the American Housecleaners Program, and has traveled extensively around the country conducting workshops and training people how to start their own housecleaning businesses. Luethy has put together practical information that is easy to read, and based on years of experience running a housecleaning business and training others to start their own. She writes "You won't have to make the same mistakes I did or go through the whole learning process because in the pages of this book I have written down everything you need to know to be an instant success."

Men and women all over are using her techniques to start their own cleaning businesses and making excellent money while enjoying excellent flexible hours along with many other benefits. Michelle Grattam of Houston, Texas is delighted with Luethy's helpful ideas: "Thanks to Rae Ann, I have more work than I know what to do with. My clients really depend on me and the money is great!"